My Love Whispers Aquarelle

Dr. Claus

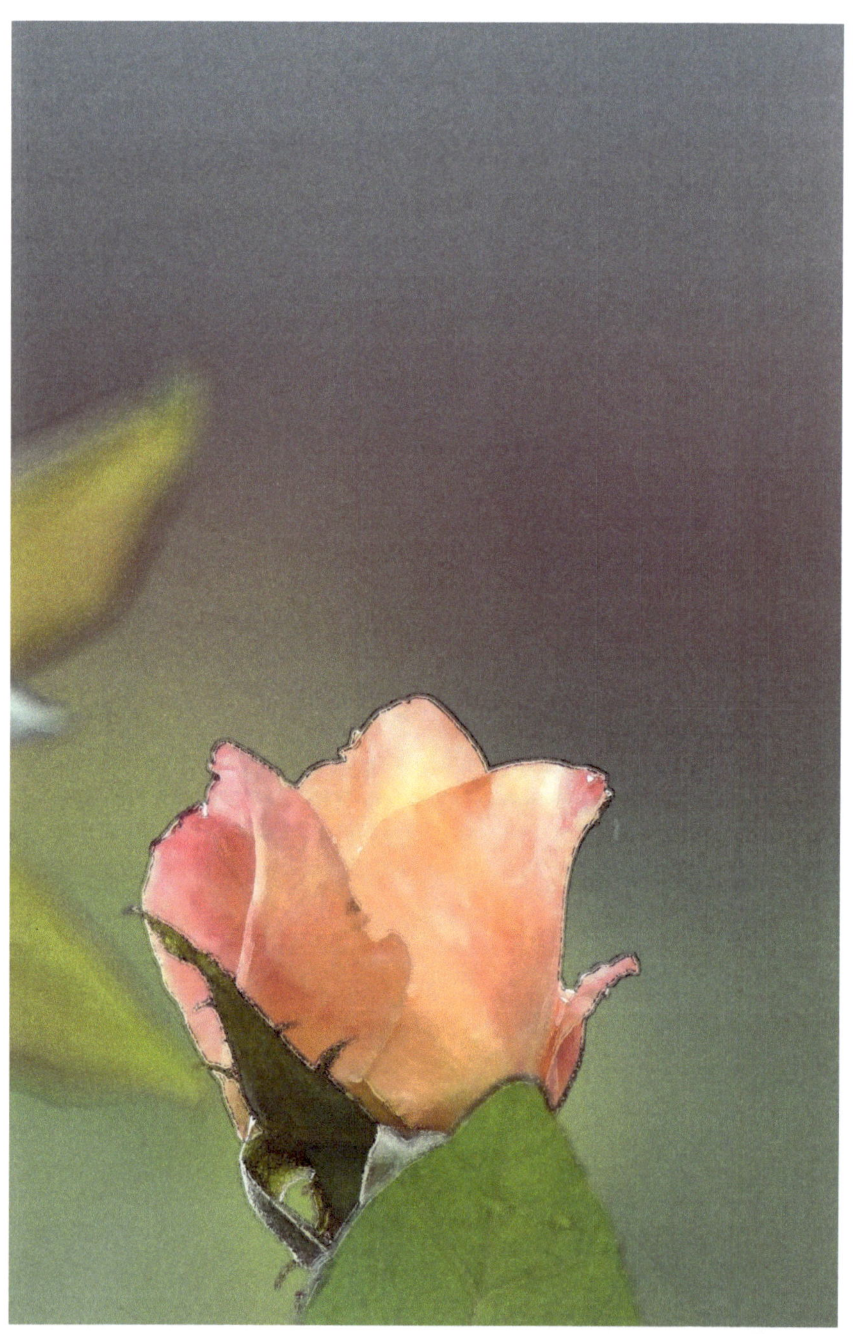

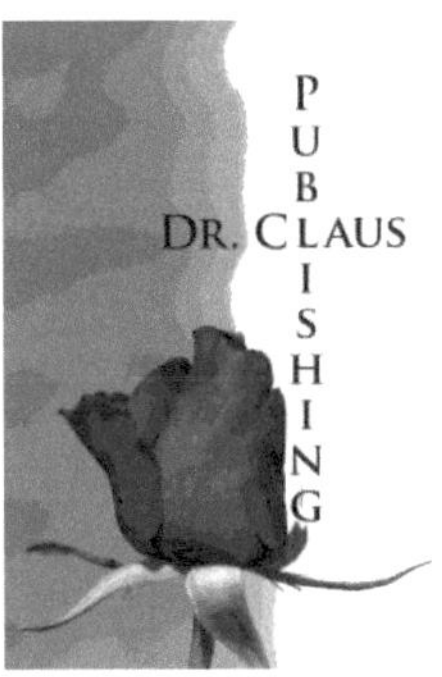

PUBLISHED BY DR. CLAUS PUBLISHING

First Edition
ISBN: 1-61497-032-7
ISBN-13: 978-1-61497-032-3
Library of Congress Control Number: 2012910864

DEDICATION

Mallory and Geoffrey

CONTENTS

ACKNOWLEDGMENT

During the war, my heart of stone was taken from my chest.
In place of that stone, I received a heart of flesh.
My old heart was handed back to me and as I received this heart of stone,
my thumbprint was forever seared into this rock.
I carry this heart of stone with me wherever I may go.
On any given day when words of doubt rain down upon my soul,
I reach for a stone once embedded in my chest
and I place my thumb into the mark.

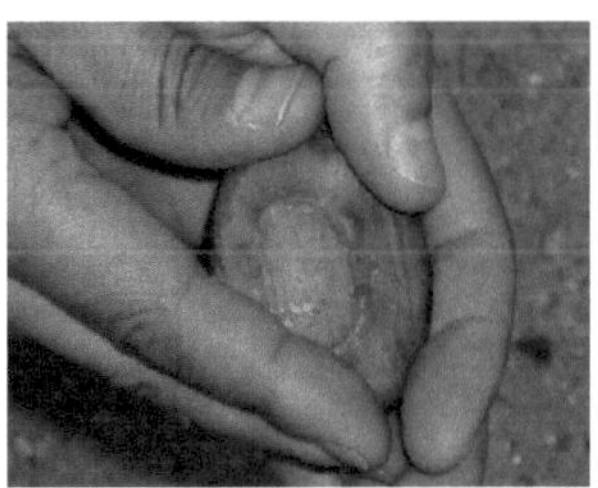

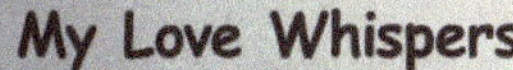

My Love Whispers

My Love you wear the rainbow
All colors touch your face
Even the gentle flowers say
From you they receive grace

My Love in all their glory
These flowers speak of you
Their beauty is your story
From your heart they all grew

They whisper Do I know you
I tell each flower this
My Love whispers I Love you
And seals it with a kiss

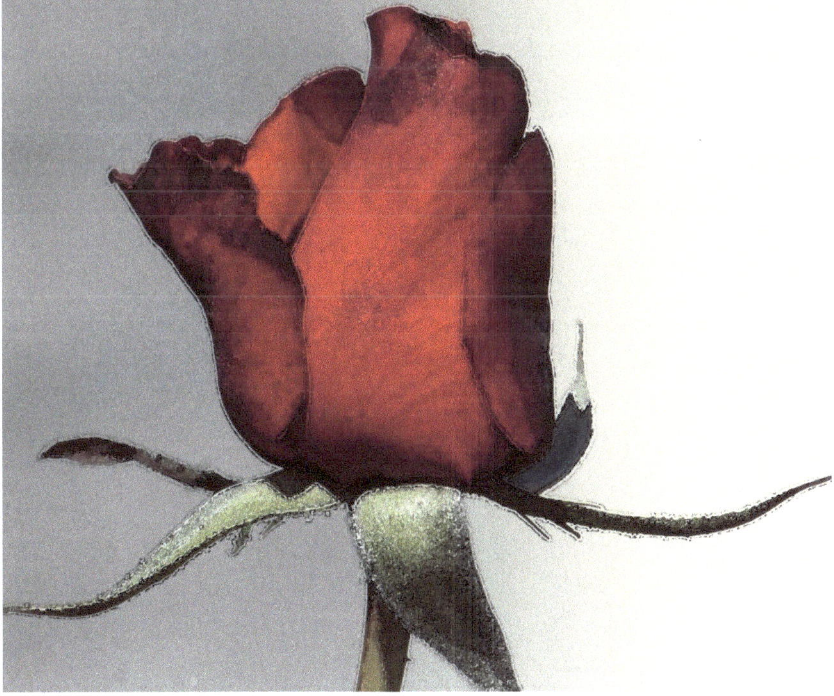

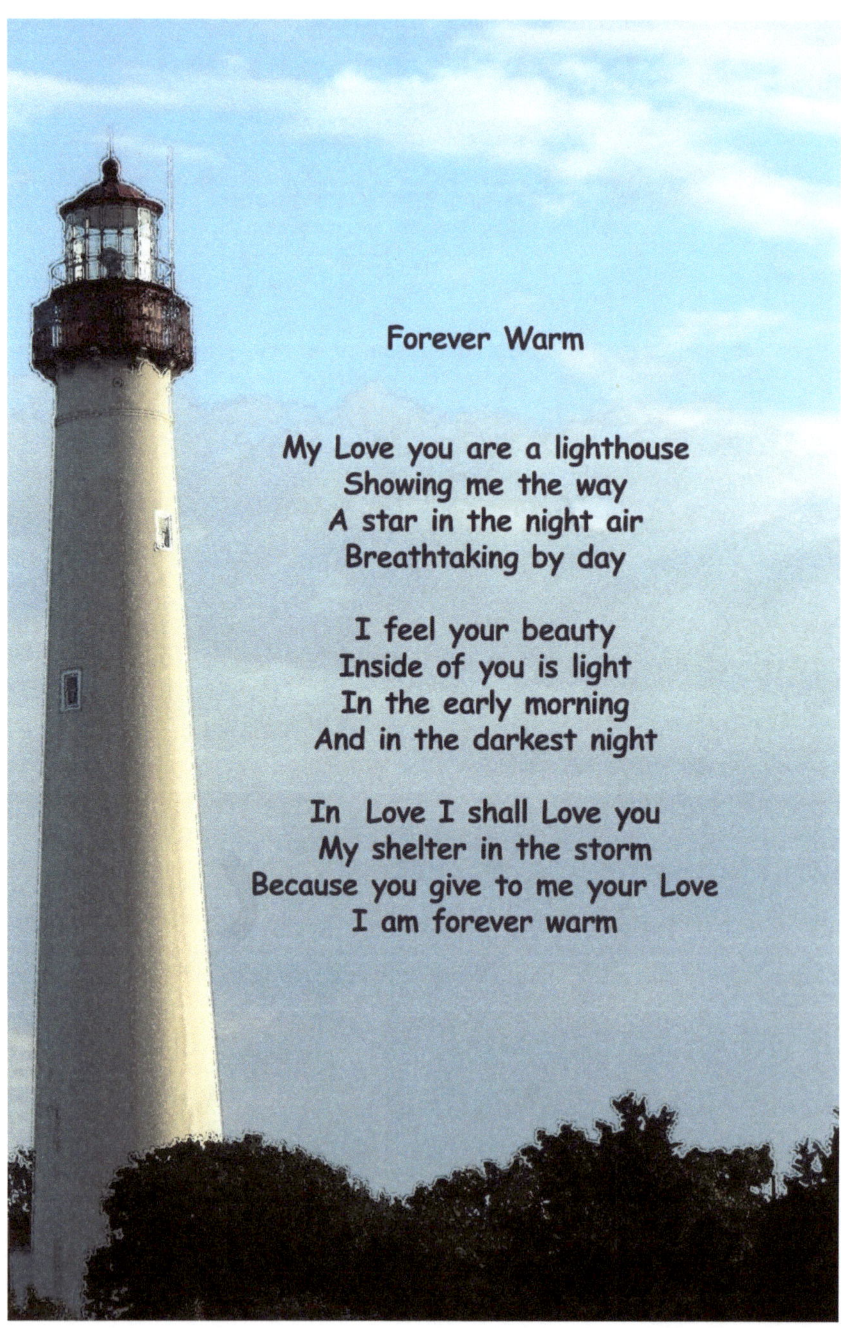

Forever Warm

My Love you are a lighthouse
Showing me the way
A star in the night air
Breathtaking by day

I feel your beauty
Inside of you is light
In the early morning
And in the darkest night

In Love I shall Love you
My shelter in the storm
Because you give to me your Love
I am forever warm

Love Will Grow

Dear Love in the garden
I gave to you my ring
For the first time in my life
I heard flowers sing

In your joy you make them glad
Their hearts fill with song
Because your smile is the sun
Their day is all night long

You are beautiful in every way
And like the flowers glow
I long to be in you each day
Where our Love will grow

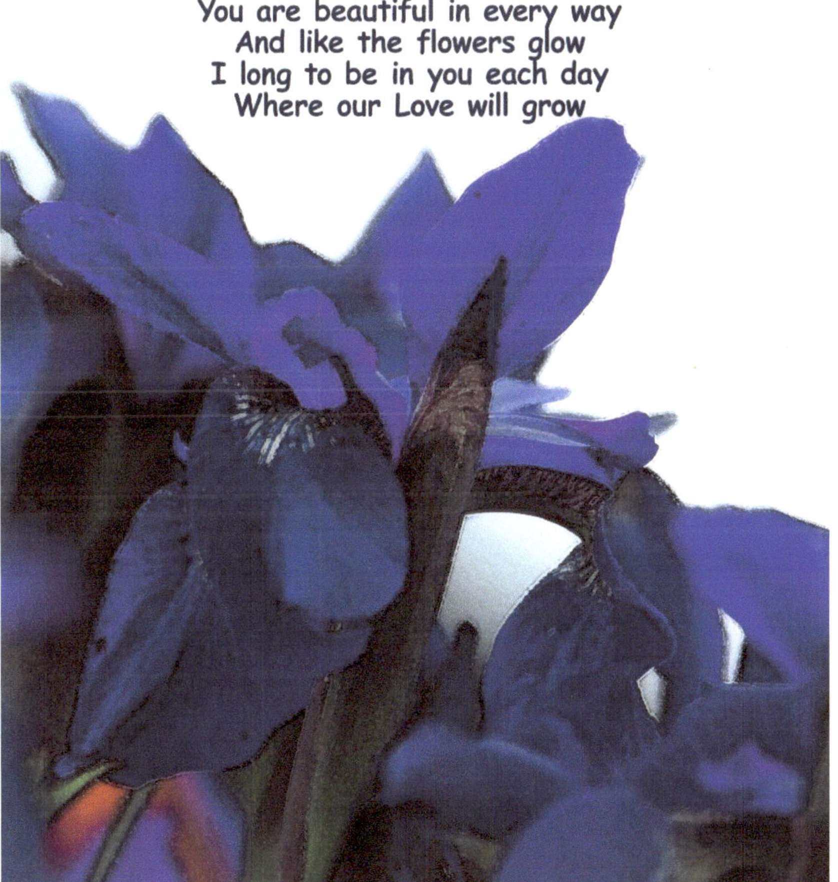

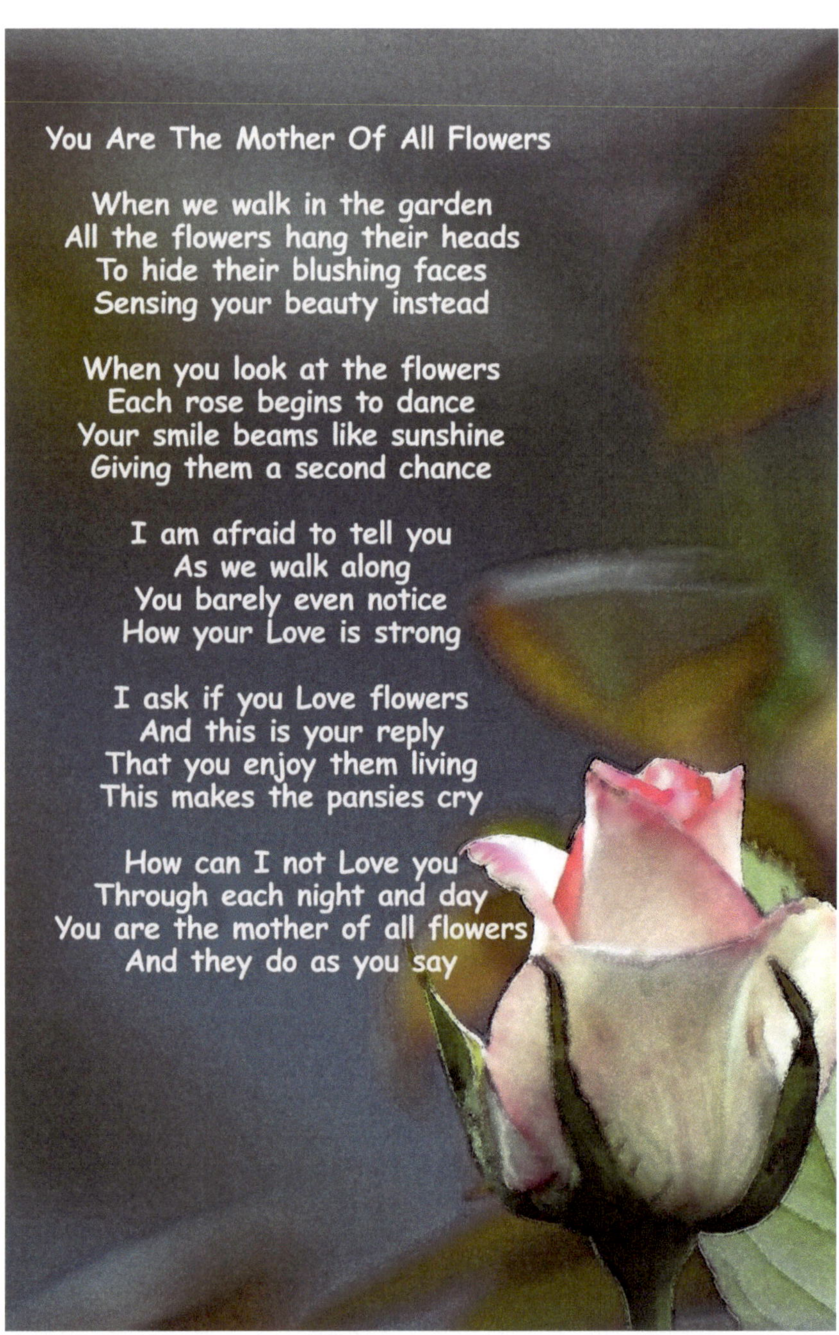

You Are The Mother Of All Flowers

When we walk in the garden
All the flowers hang their heads
To hide their blushing faces
Sensing your beauty instead

When you look at the flowers
Each rose begins to dance
Your smile beams like sunshine
Giving them a second chance

I am afraid to tell you
As we walk along
You barely even notice
How your Love is strong

I ask if you Love flowers
And this is your reply
That you enjoy them living
This makes the pansies cry

How can I not Love you
Through each night and day
You are the mother of all flowers
And they do as you say

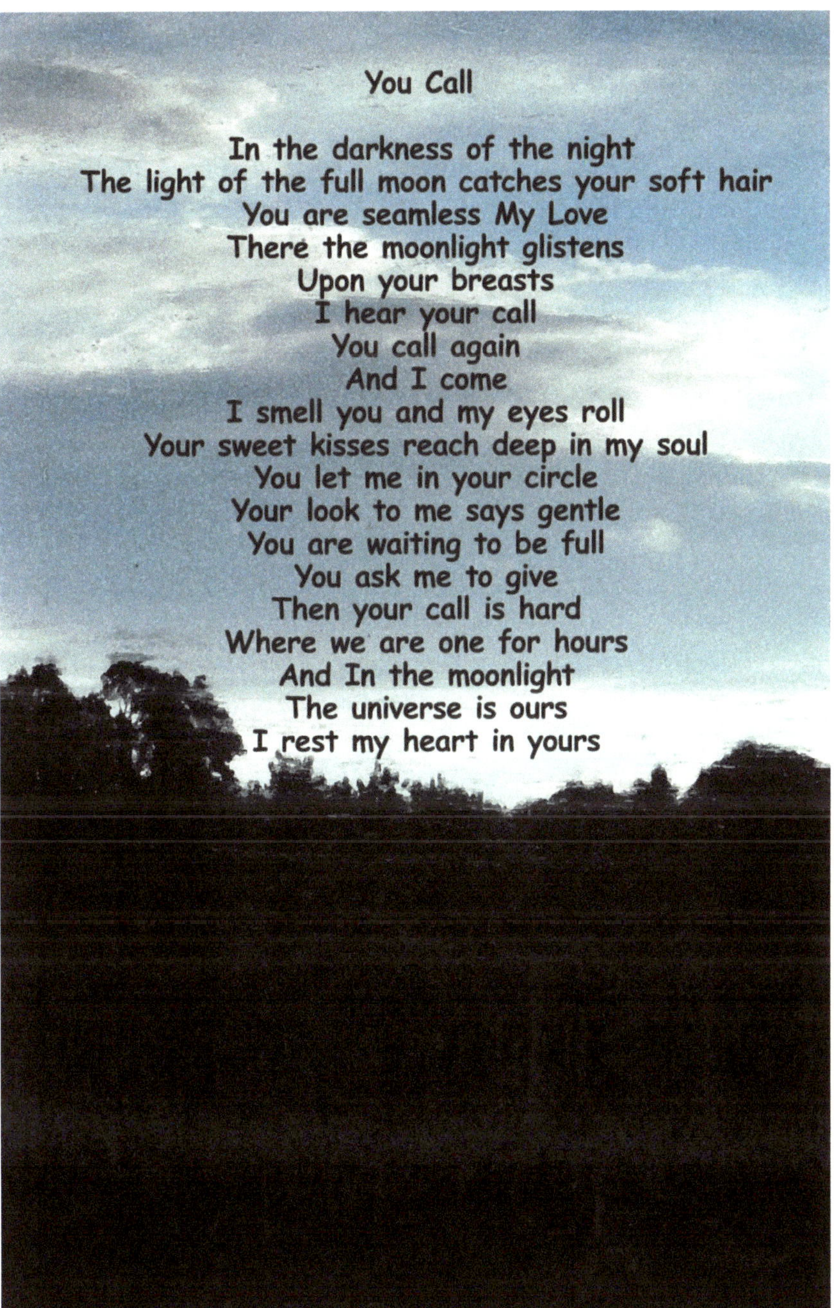

You Call

In the darkness of the night
The light of the full moon catches your soft hair
You are seamless My Love
There the moonlight glistens
Upon your breasts
I hear your call
You call again
And I come
I smell you and my eyes roll
Your sweet kisses reach deep in my soul
You let me in your circle
Your look to me says gentle
You are waiting to be full
You ask me to give
Then your call is hard
Where we are one for hours
And In the moonlight
The universe is ours
I rest my heart in yours

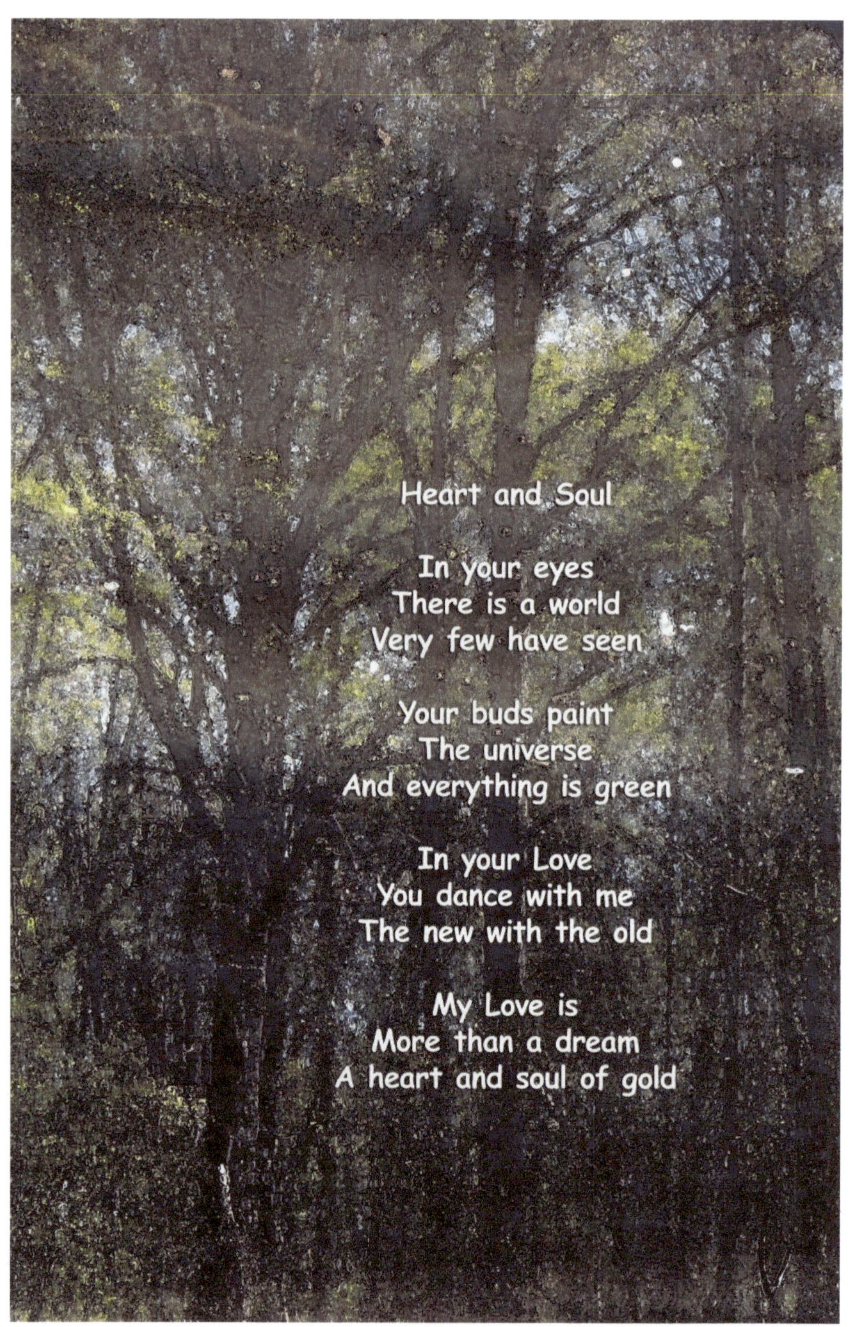

Heart and Soul

In your eyes
There is a world
Very few have seen

Your buds paint
The universe
And everything is green

In your Love
You dance with me
The new with the old

My Love is
More than a dream
A heart and soul of gold

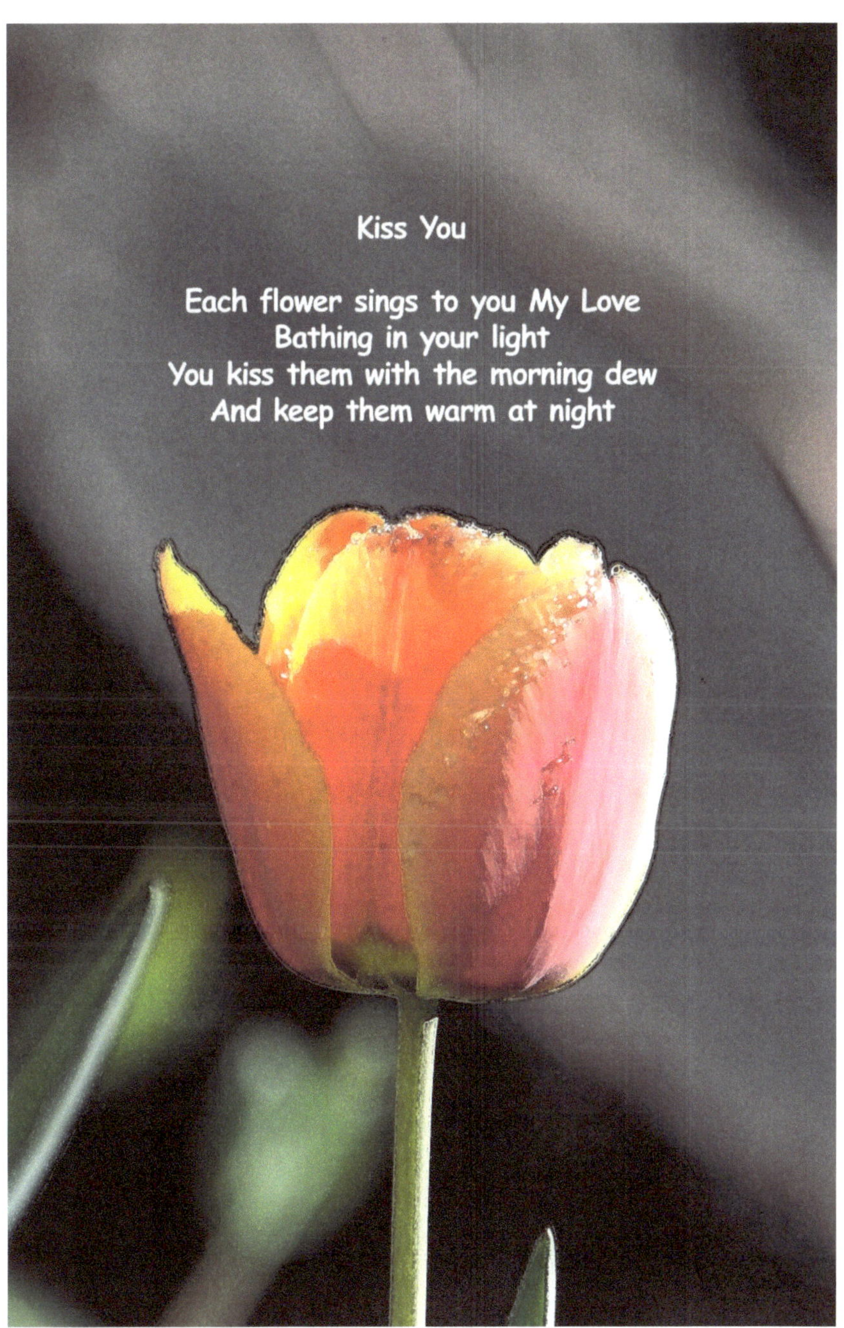
Kiss You

Each flower sings to you My Love
Bathing in your light
You kiss them with the morning dew
And keep them warm at night

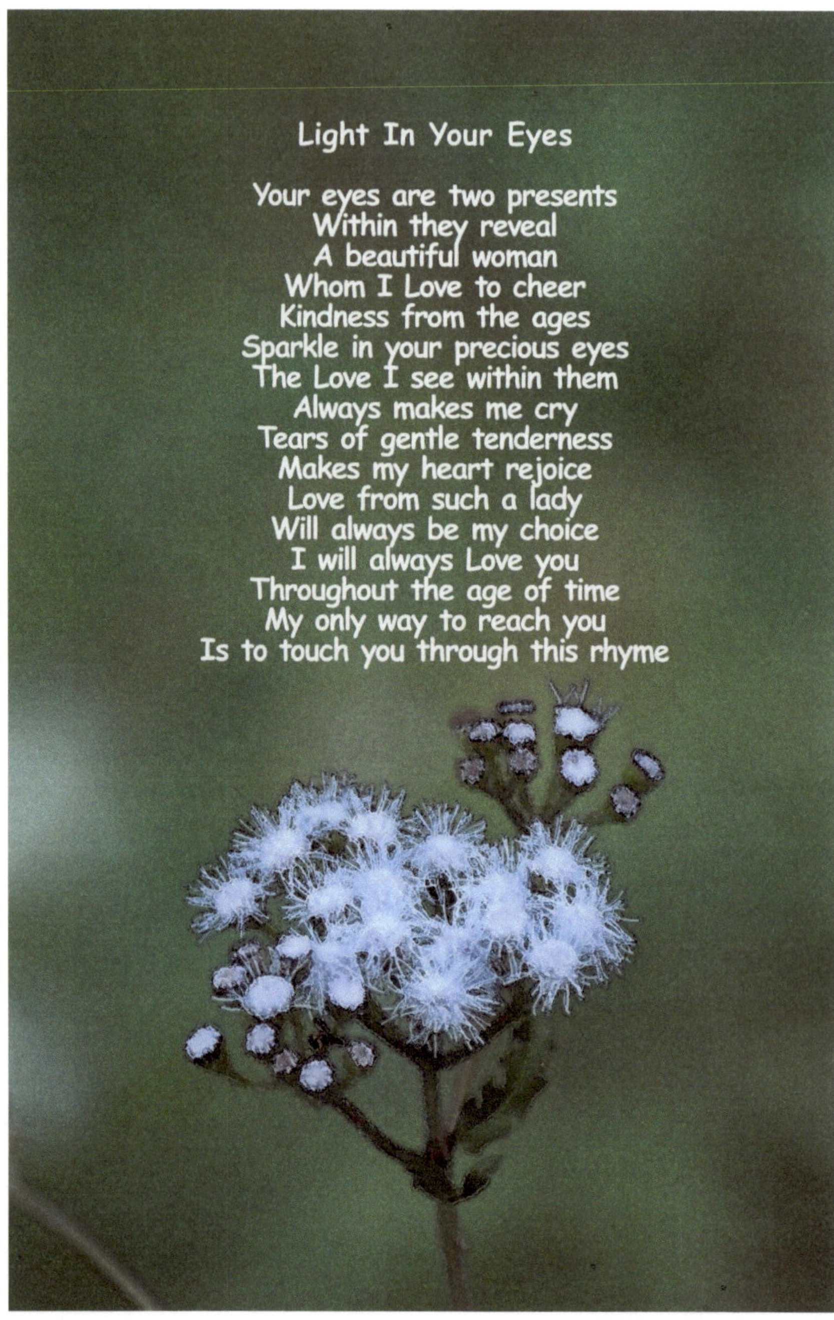

Light In Your Eyes

Your eyes are two presents
Within they reveal
A beautiful woman
Whom I Love to cheer
Kindness from the ages
Sparkle in your precious eyes
The Love I see within them
Always makes me cry
Tears of gentle tenderness
Makes my heart rejoice
Love from such a lady
Will always be my choice
I will always Love you
Throughout the age of time
My only way to reach you
Is to touch you through this rhyme

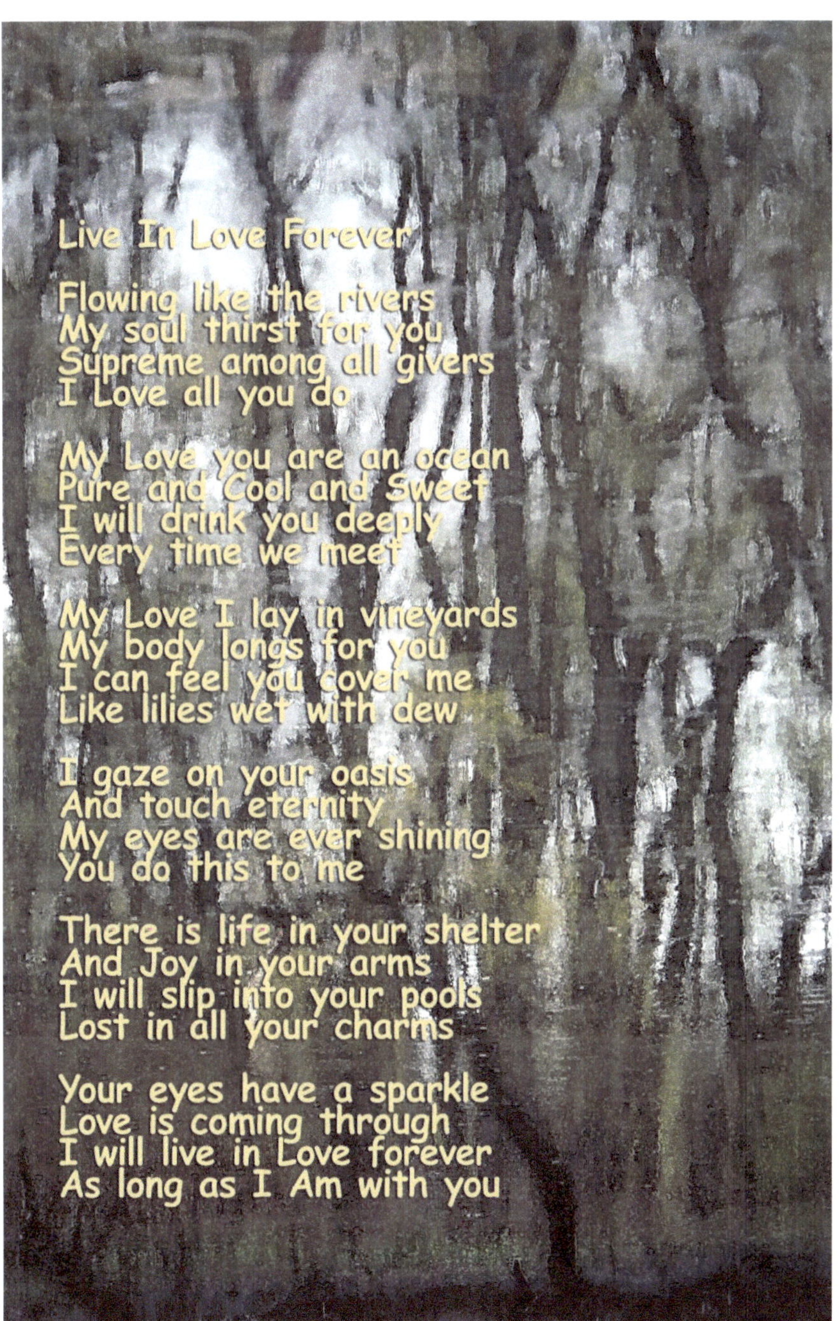
Live In Love Forever

Flowing like the rivers
My soul thirst for you
Supreme among all givers
I Love all you do

My Love you are an ocean
Pure and Cool and Sweet
I will drink you deeply
Every time we meet

My Love I lay in vineyards
My body longs for you
I can feel you cover me
Like lilies wet with dew

I gaze on your oasis
And touch eternity
My eyes are ever shining
You do this to me

There is life in your shelter
And Joy in your arms
I will slip into your pools
Lost in all your charms

Your eyes have a sparkle
Love is coming through
I will live in Love forever
As long as I Am with you

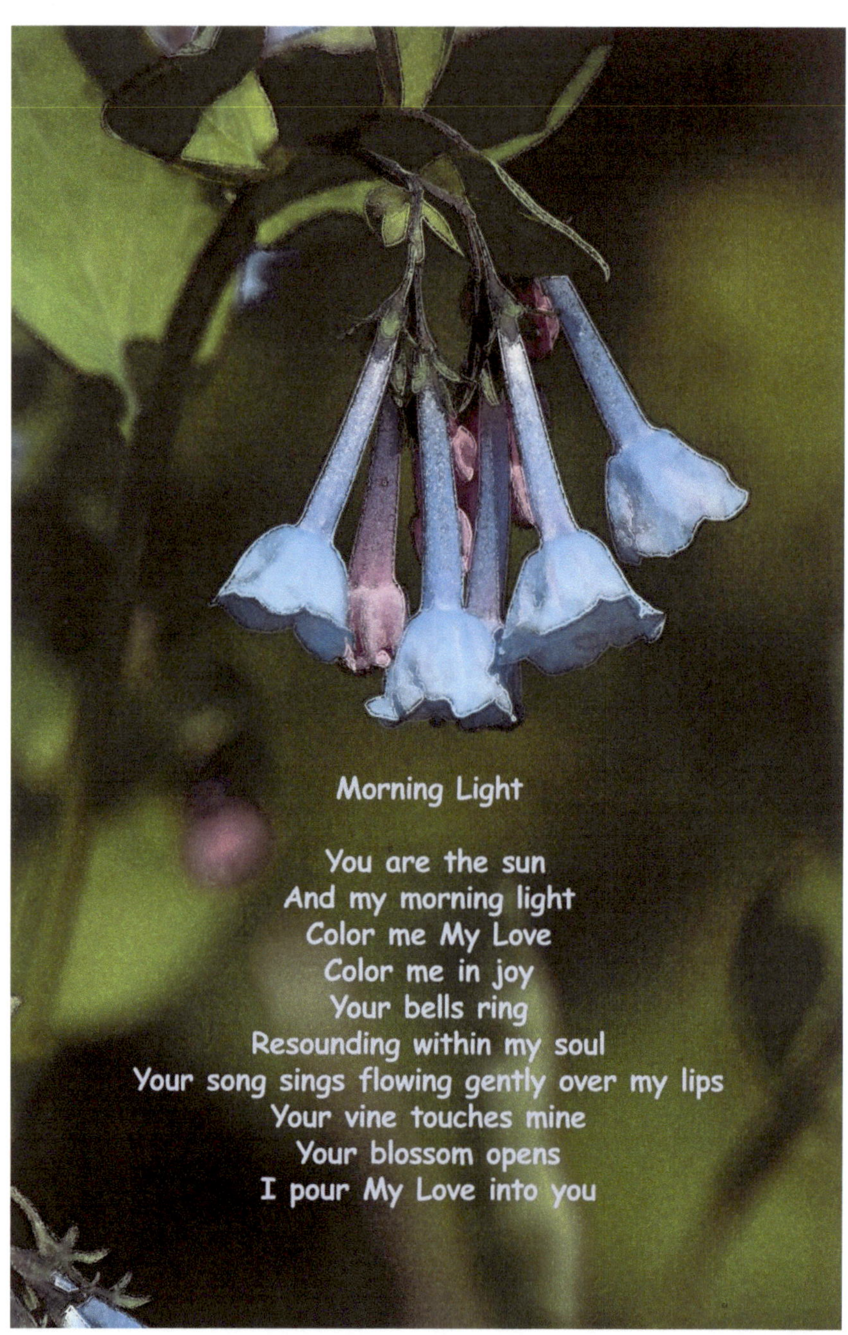

Morning Light

You are the sun
And my morning light
Color me My Love
Color me in joy
Your bells ring
Resounding within my soul
Your song sings flowing gently over my lips
Your vine touches mine
Your blossom opens
I pour My Love into you

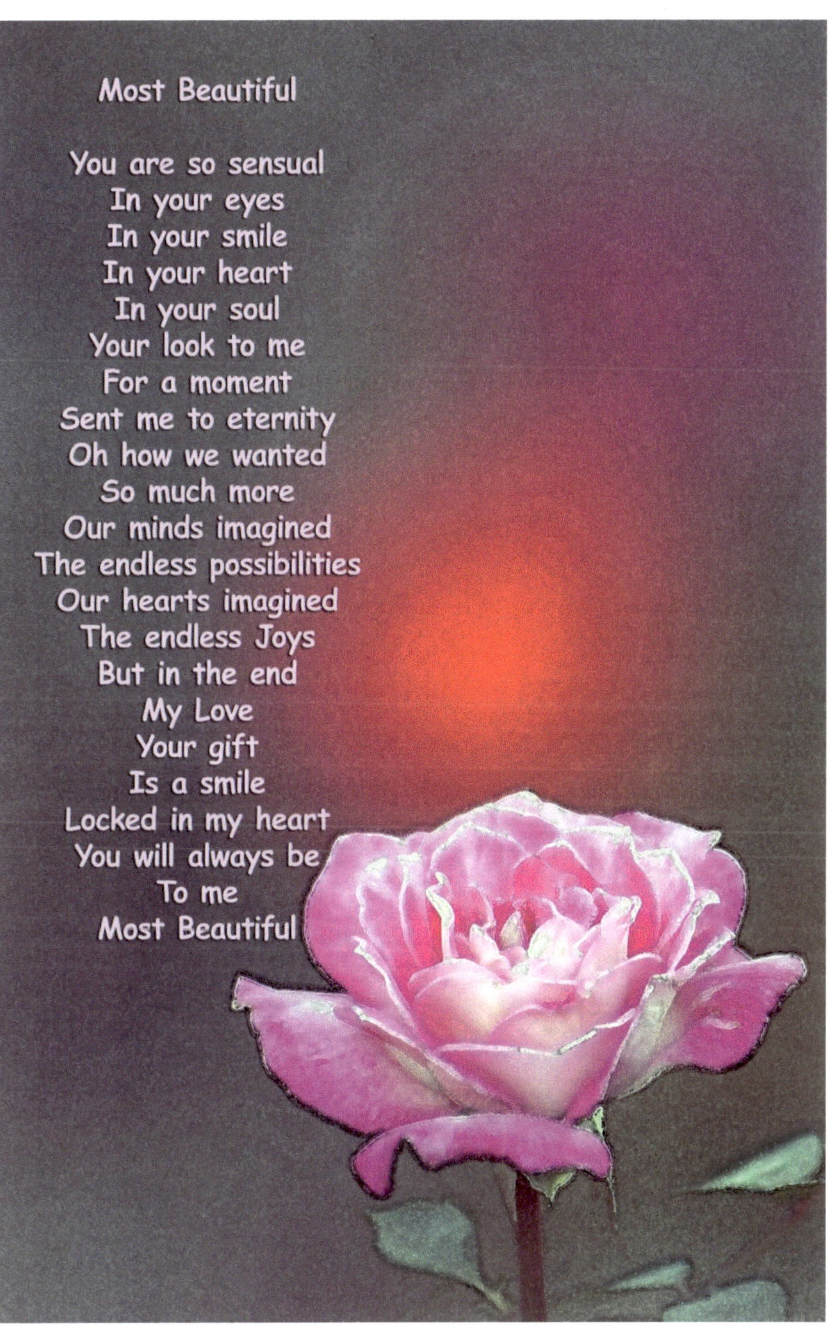
Most Beautiful

You are so sensual
In your eyes
In your smile
In your heart
In your soul
Your look to me
For a moment
Sent me to eternity
Oh how we wanted
So much more
Our minds imagined
The endless possibilities
Our hearts imagined
The endless Joys
But in the end
My Love
Your gift
Is a smile
Locked in my heart
You will always be
To me
Most Beautiful

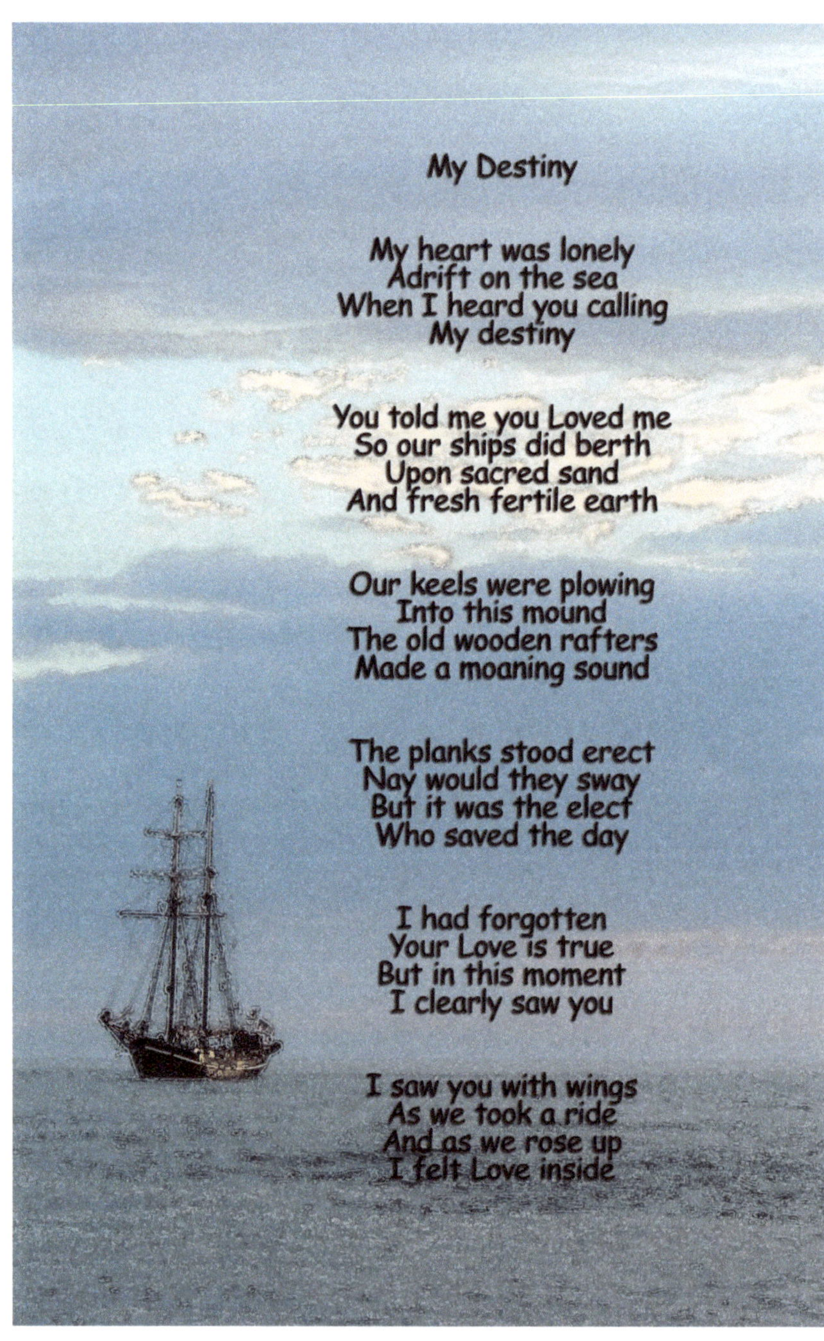

My Destiny

My heart was lonely
Adrift on the sea
When I heard you calling
My destiny

You told me you Loved me
So our ships did berth
Upon sacred sand
And fresh fertile earth

Our keels were plowing
Into this mound
The old wooden rafters
Made a moaning sound

The planks stood erect
Nay would they sway
But it was the elect
Who saved the day

I had forgotten
Your Love is true
But in this moment
I clearly saw you

I saw you with wings
As we took a ride
And as we rose up
I felt Love inside

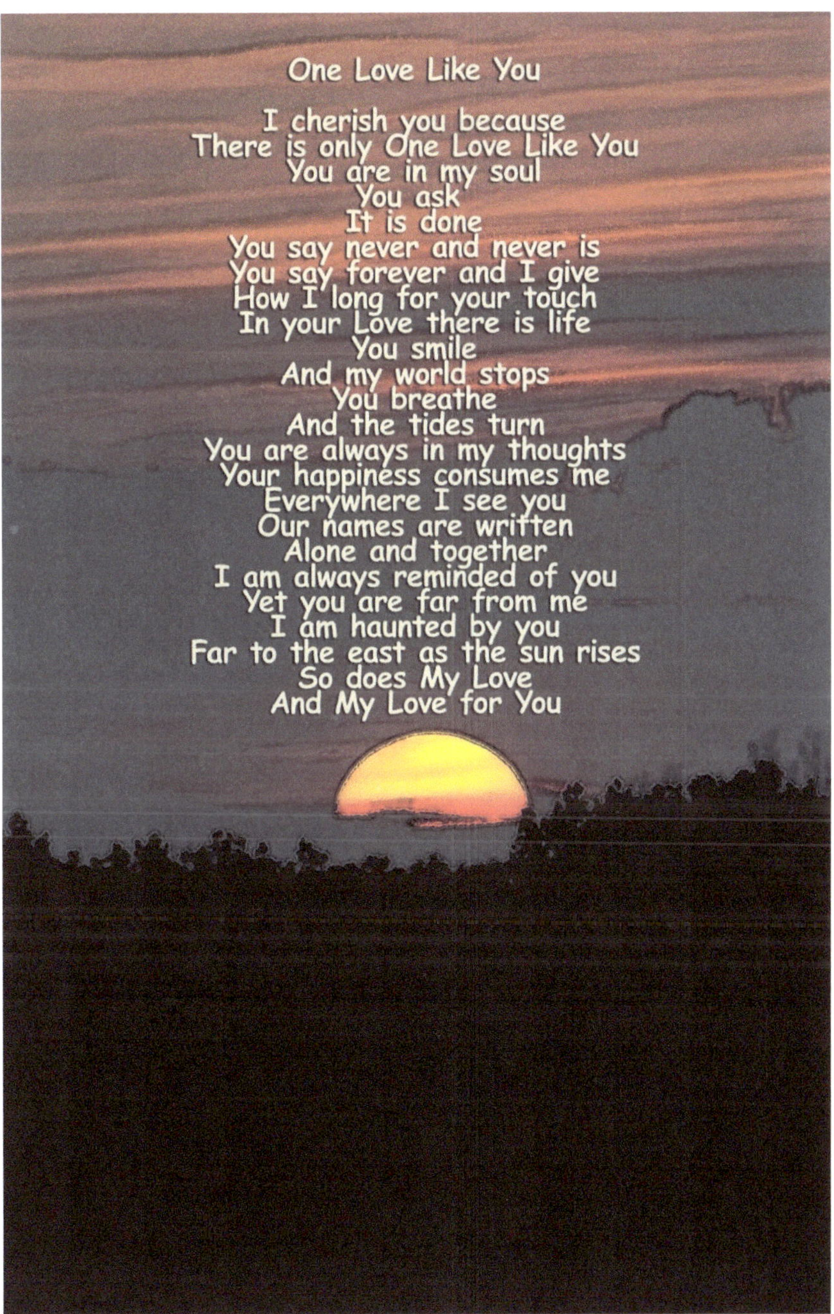
One Love Like You
I cherish you because
There is only One Love Like You
You are in my soul
You ask
It is done
You say never and never is
You say forever and I give
How I long for your touch
In your Love there is life
You smile
And my world stops
You breathe
And the tides turn
You are always in my thoughts
Your happiness consumes me
Everywhere I see you
Our names are written
Alone and together
I am always reminded of you
Yet you are far from me
I am haunted by you
Far to the east as the sun rises
So does My Love
And My Love for You

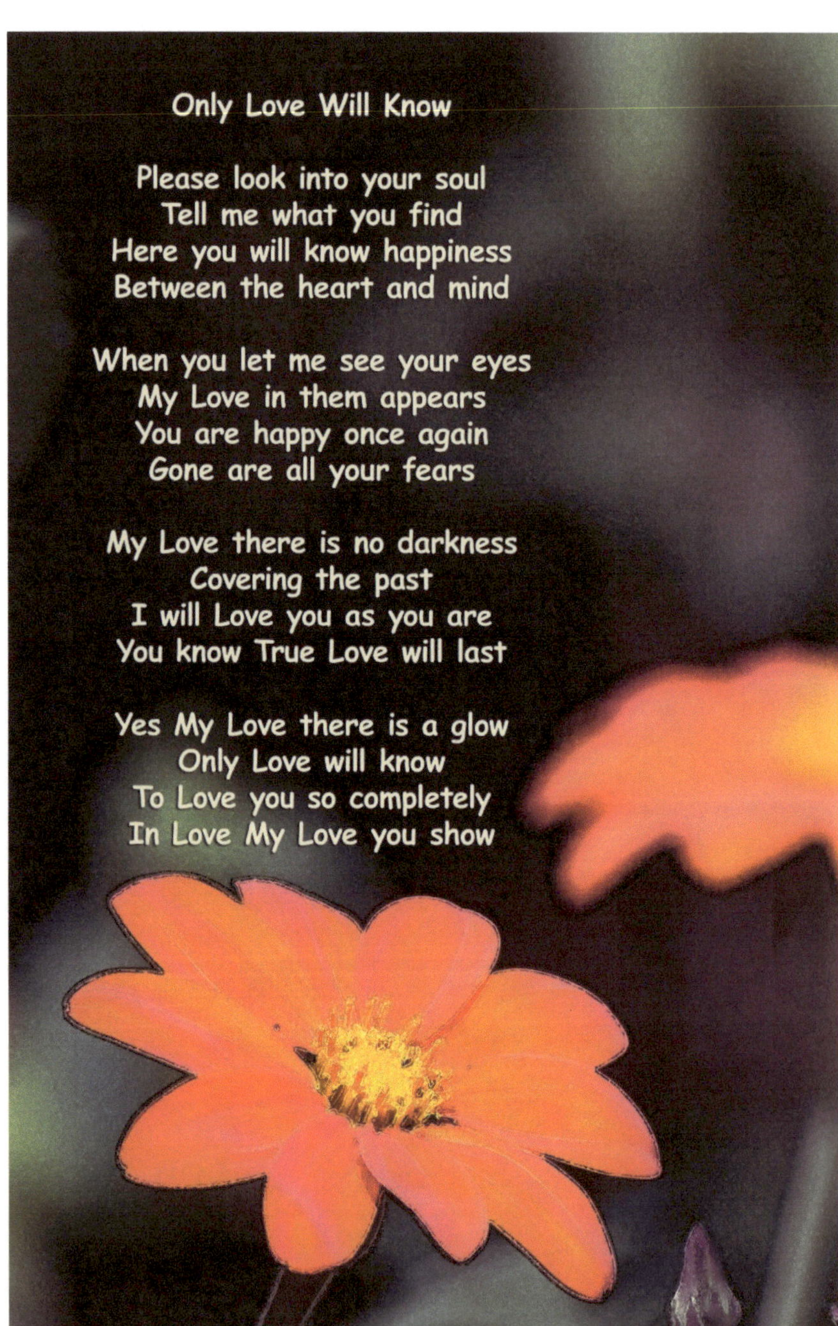
Only Love Will Know

Please look into your soul
Tell me what you find
Here you will know happiness
Between the heart and mind

When you let me see your eyes
My Love in them appears
You are happy once again
Gone are all your fears

My Love there is no darkness
Covering the past
I will Love you as you are
You know True Love will last

Yes My Love there is a glow
Only Love will know
To Love you so completely
In Love My Love you show

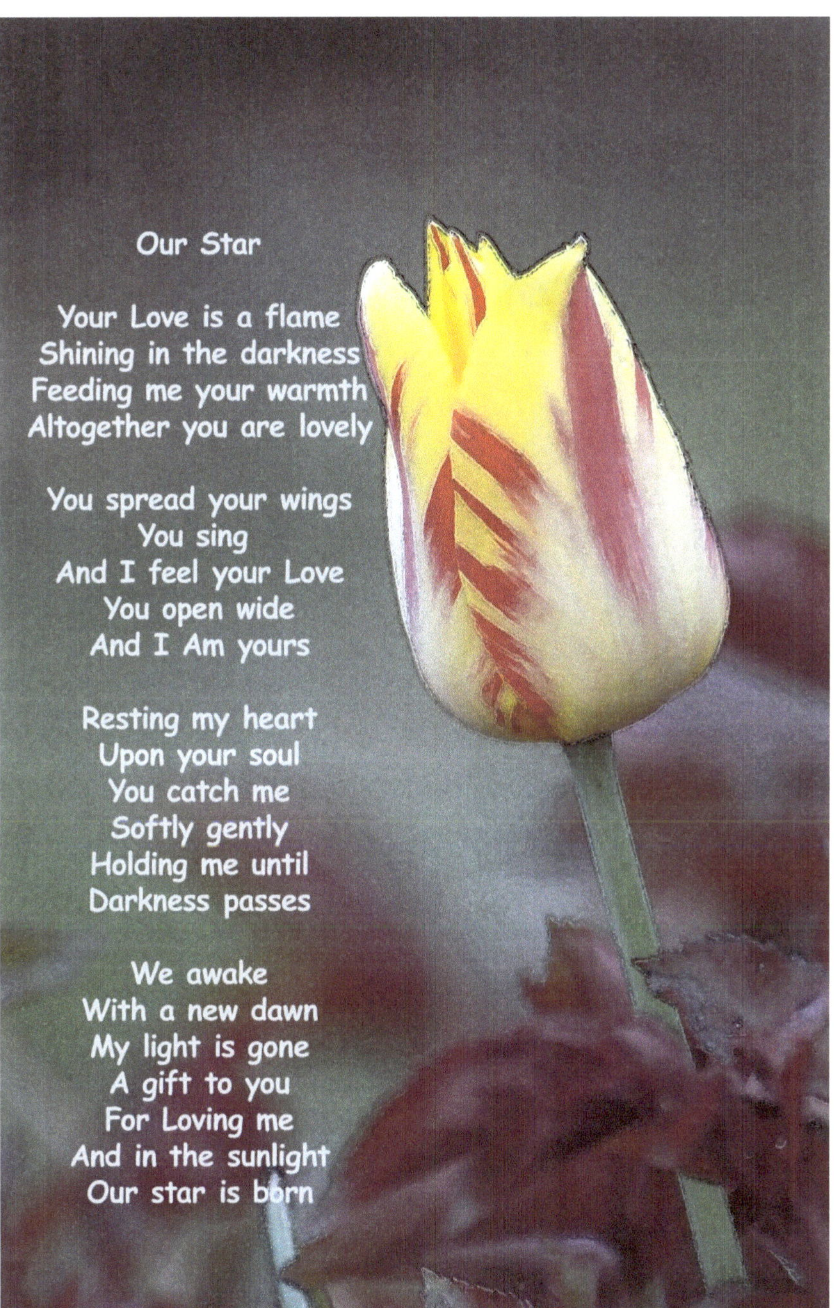
Our Star

Your Love is a flame
Shining in the darkness
Feeding me your warmth
Altogether you are lovely

You spread your wings
You sing
And I feel your Love
You open wide
And I Am yours

Resting my heart
Upon your soul
You catch me
Softly gently
Holding me until
Darkness passes

We awake
With a new dawn
My light is gone
A gift to you
For Loving me
And in the sunlight
Our star is born

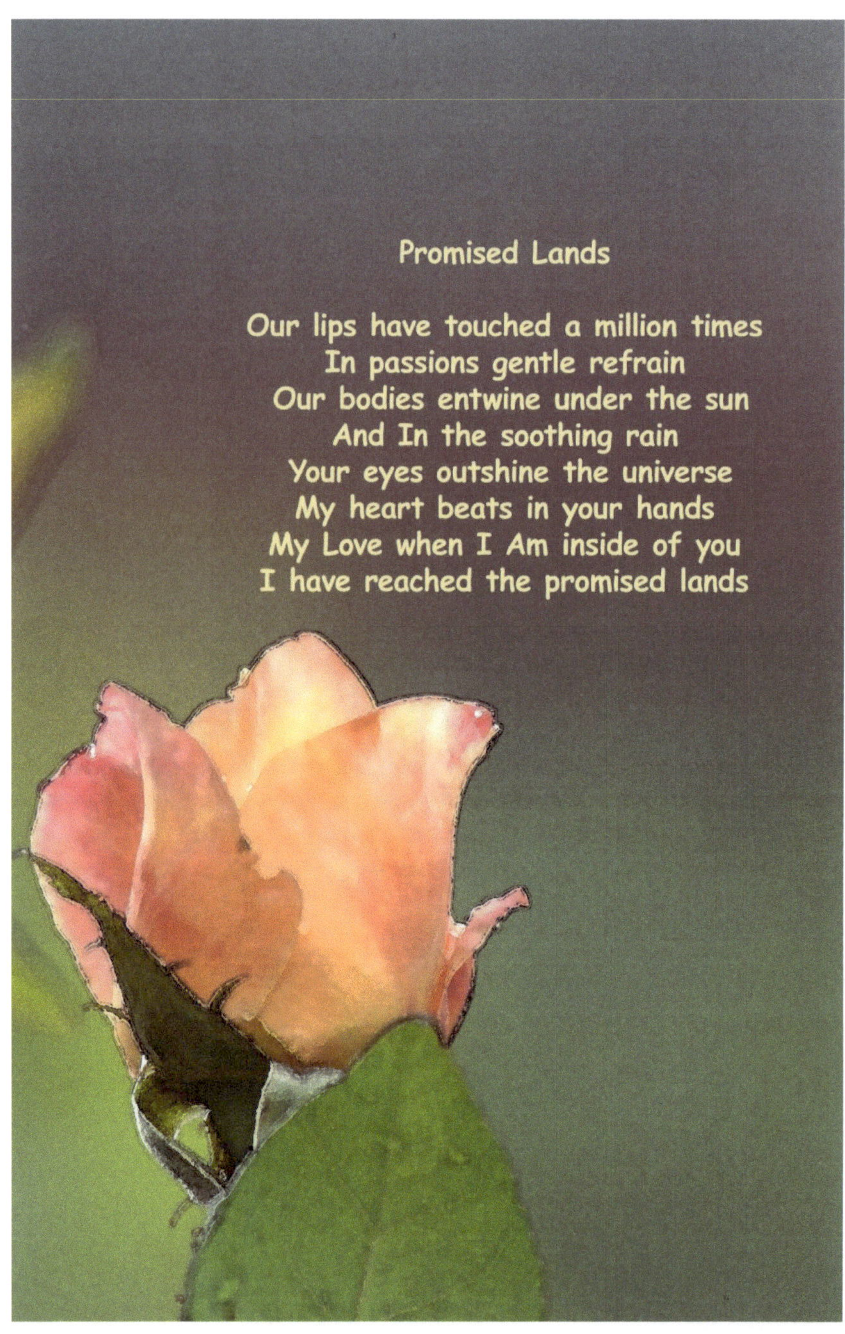

Promised Lands

Our lips have touched a million times
In passions gentle refrain
Our bodies entwine under the sun
And In the soothing rain
Your eyes outshine the universe
My heart beats in your hands
My Love when I Am inside of you
I have reached the promised lands

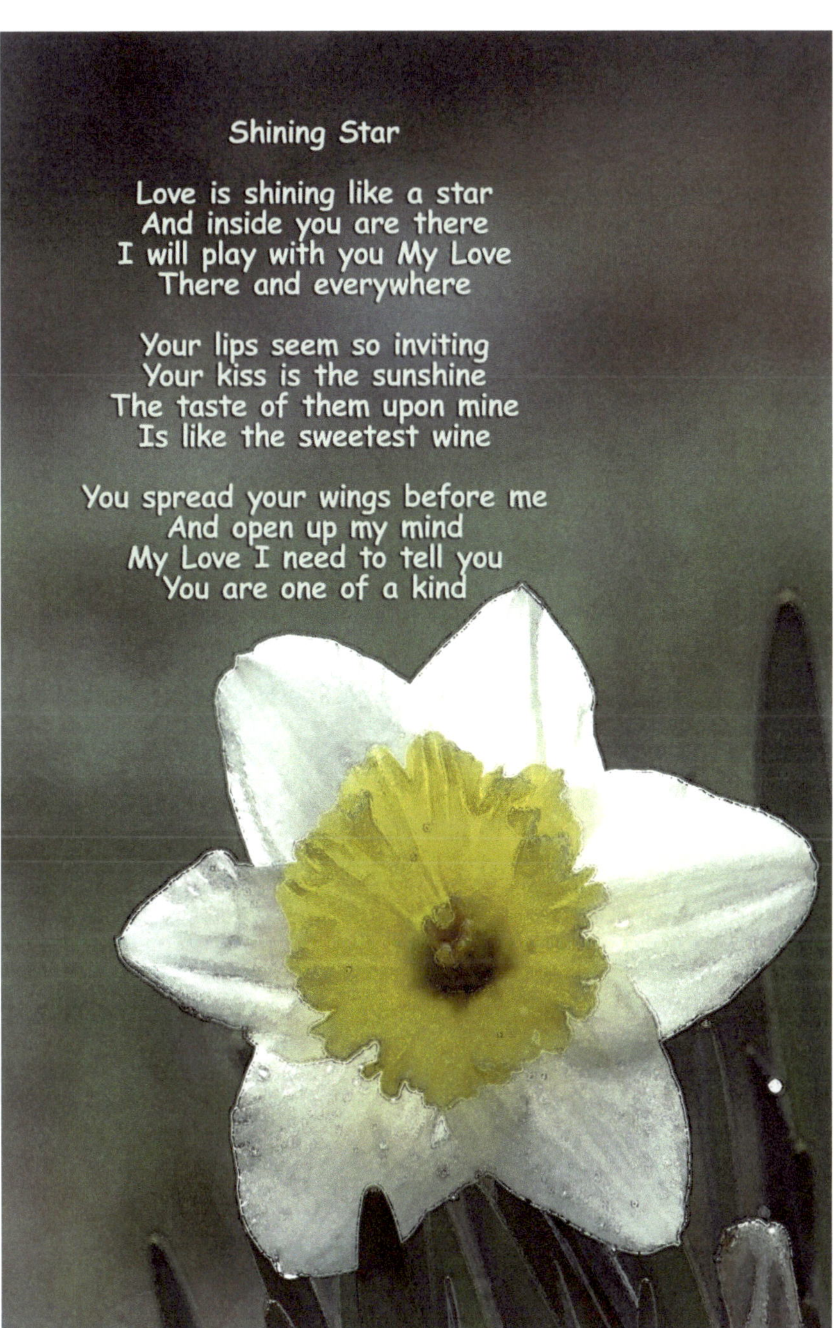
Shining Star

Love is shining like a star
And inside you are there
I will play with you My Love
There and everywhere

Your lips seem so inviting
Your kiss is the sunshine
The taste of them upon mine
Is like the sweetest wine

You spread your wings before me
And open up my mind
My Love I need to tell you
You are one of a kind

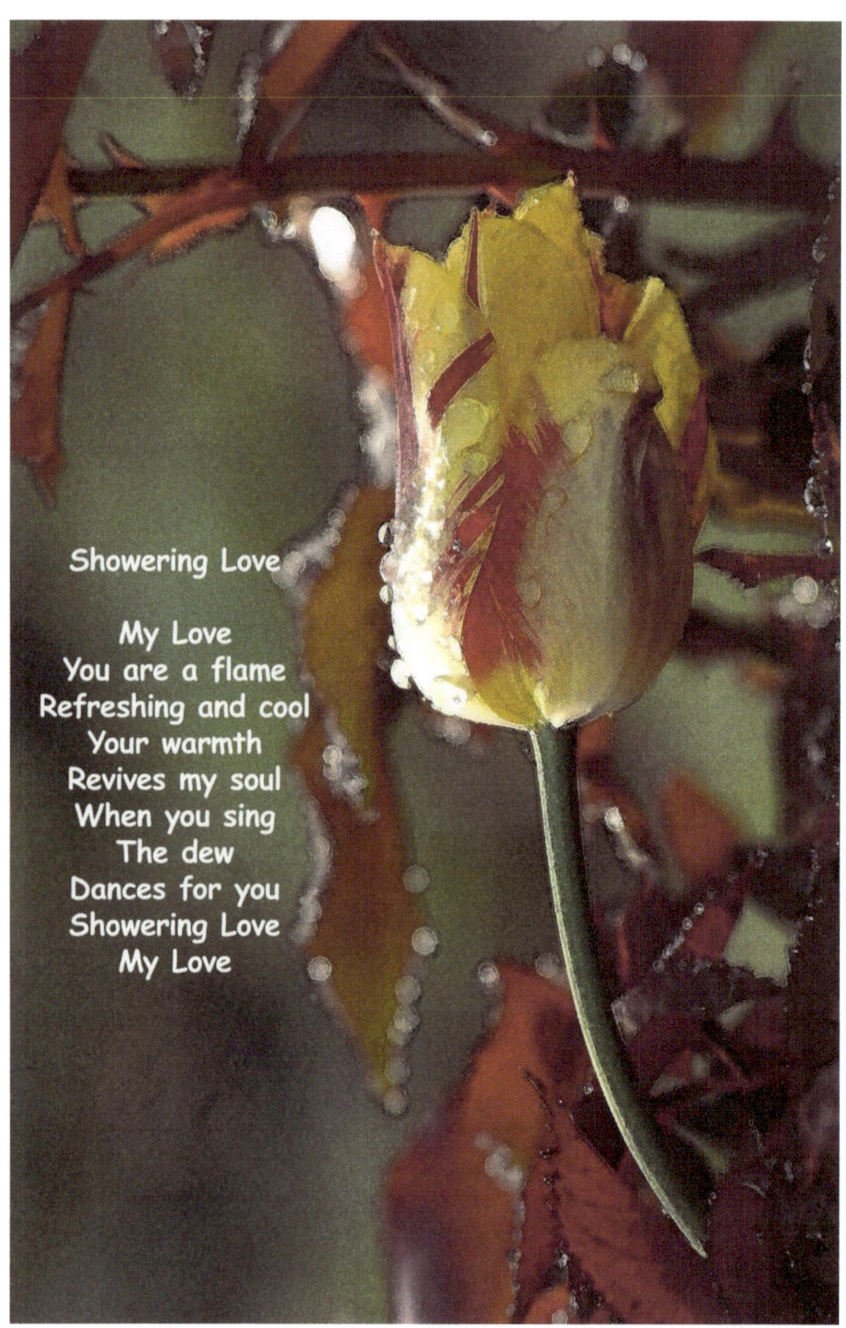
Showering Love

My Love
You are a flame
Refreshing and cool
Your warmth
Revives my soul
When you sing
The dew
Dances for you
Showering Love
My Love

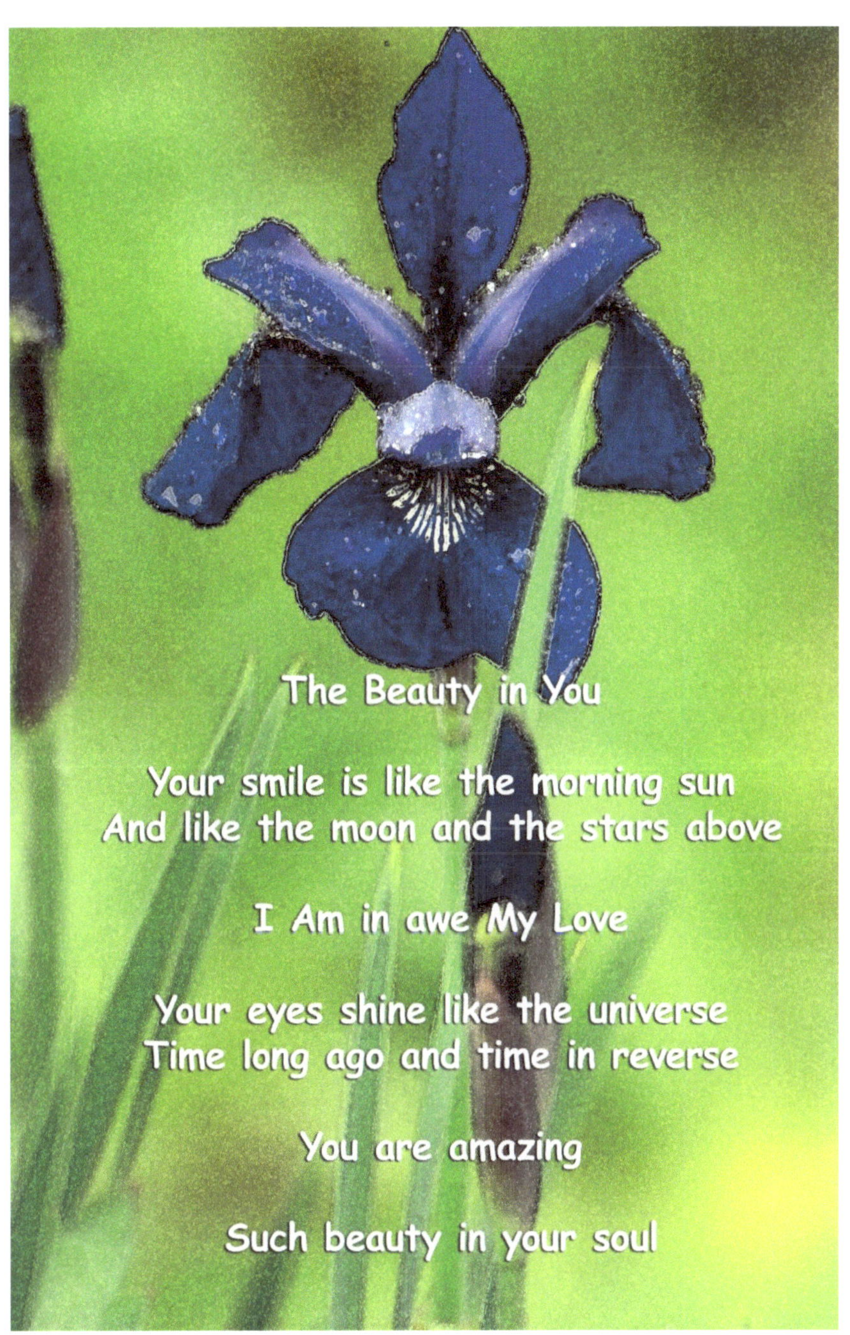

The Beauty in You

Your smile is like the morning sun
And like the moon and the stars above

I Am in awe My Love

Your eyes shine like the universe
Time long ago and time in reverse

You are amazing

Such beauty in your soul

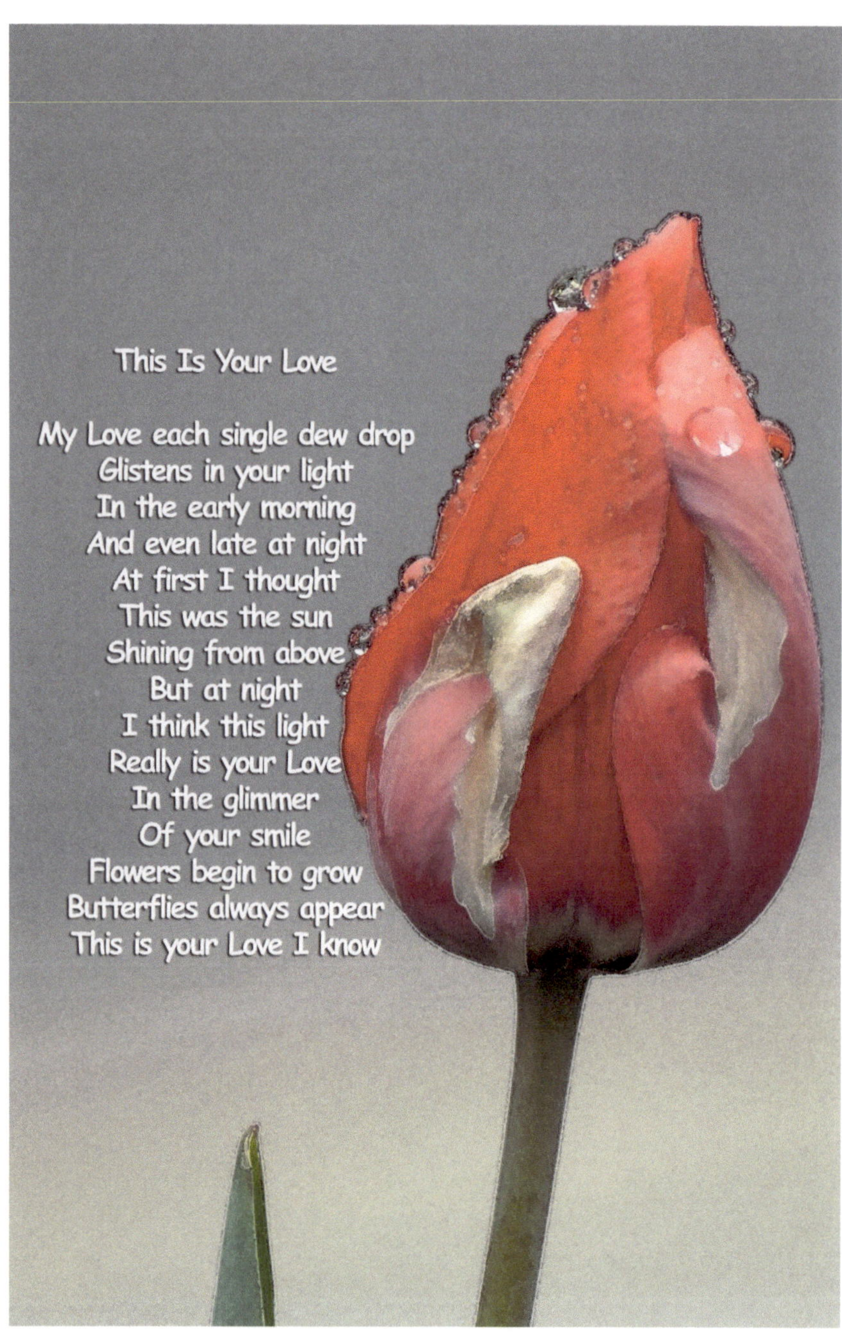
This Is Your Love

My Love each single dew drop
Glistens in your light
In the early morning
And even late at night
At first I thought
This was the sun
Shining from above
But at night
I think this light
Really is your Love
In the glimmer
Of your smile
Flowers begin to grow
Butterflies always appear
This is your Love I know

Three Tiny Words

I share with you
The beauty I see
Within your soul
Shining through your eyes
For a moment you laugh
You are flying My Love
On the wings of the wind
Truth is your scepter
Your fortress is mighty
Solid around your heart
You are safe
But I feel your loneliness
So am I
I climb your castle walls
Whispering as I go
The only gift I have
All the poems asleep in my heart
Hoping your Love will grow
You become angry My Love
I am getting close
You choose not to hurt again
So you hurt me
You mention forever
And dash me to the rocks below
The fall is great
But My Love your Love is greater
I could die
My lungs are bursting
My heart is bleeding
I hold on to one hope
Three tiny words
But together they are greater
Than all of time
Put together
Your Love at once
Is like the air I breathe
Your smile is The morning sun
Your kiss is full of life
Your eyes reveal the universe
You are my shelter
And my strength
My Love and
My weakness
I hear you say to me
I LOVE YOU
Your Love is all I have now
And your Love is all I need
You Love me
I know nothing greater
I Love you too
So I sing to you My Love...Everyday
Hoping to hear you say
I Love You
Once Again

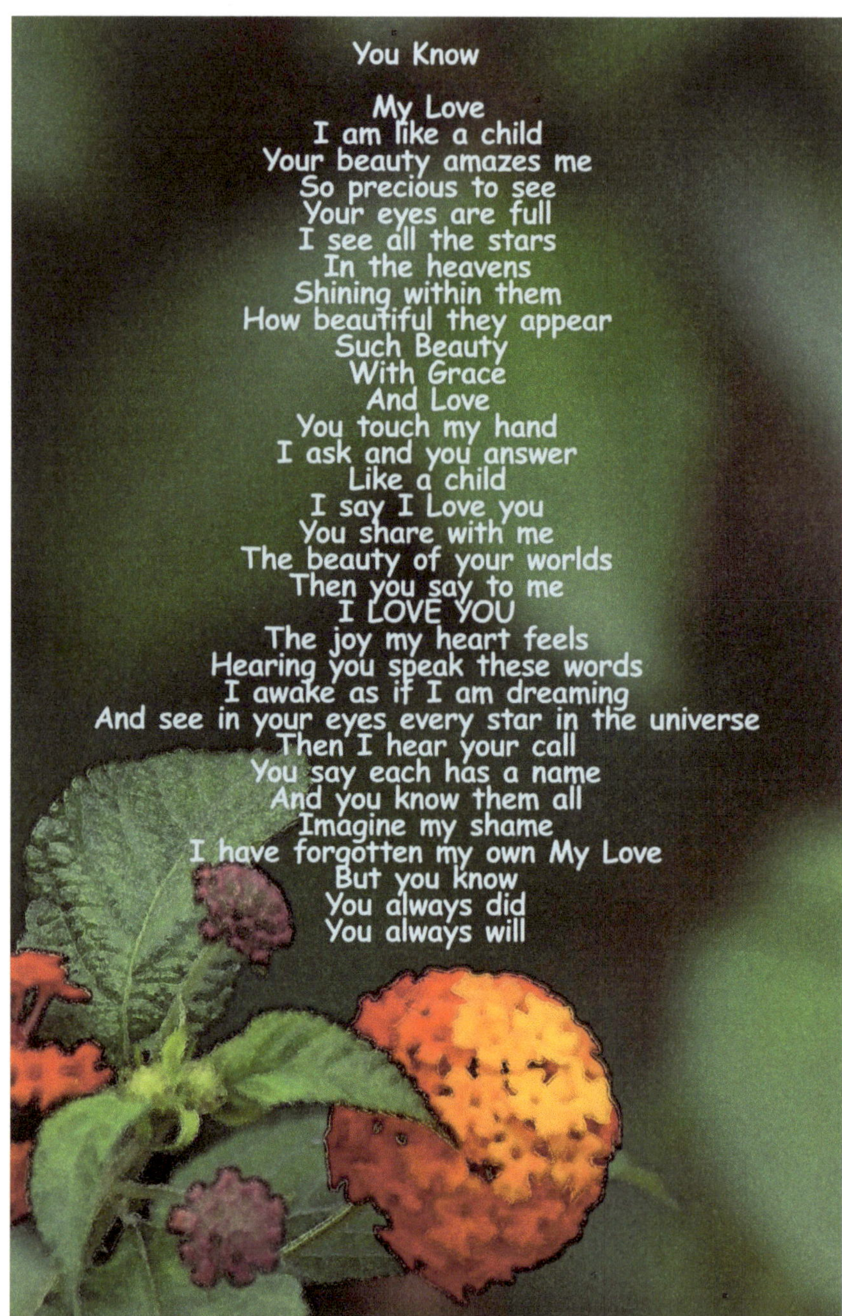

You Know

My Love
I am like a child
Your beauty amazes me
So precious to see
Your eyes are full
I see all the stars
In the heavens
Shining within them
How beautiful they appear
Such Beauty
With Grace
And Love
You touch my hand
I ask and you answer
Like a child
I say I Love you
You share with me
The beauty of your worlds
Then you say to me
I LOVE YOU
The joy my heart feels
Hearing you speak these words
I awake as if I am dreaming
And see in your eyes every star in the universe
Then I hear your call
You say each has a name
And you know them all
Imagine my shame
I have forgotten my own My Love
But you know
You always did
You always will

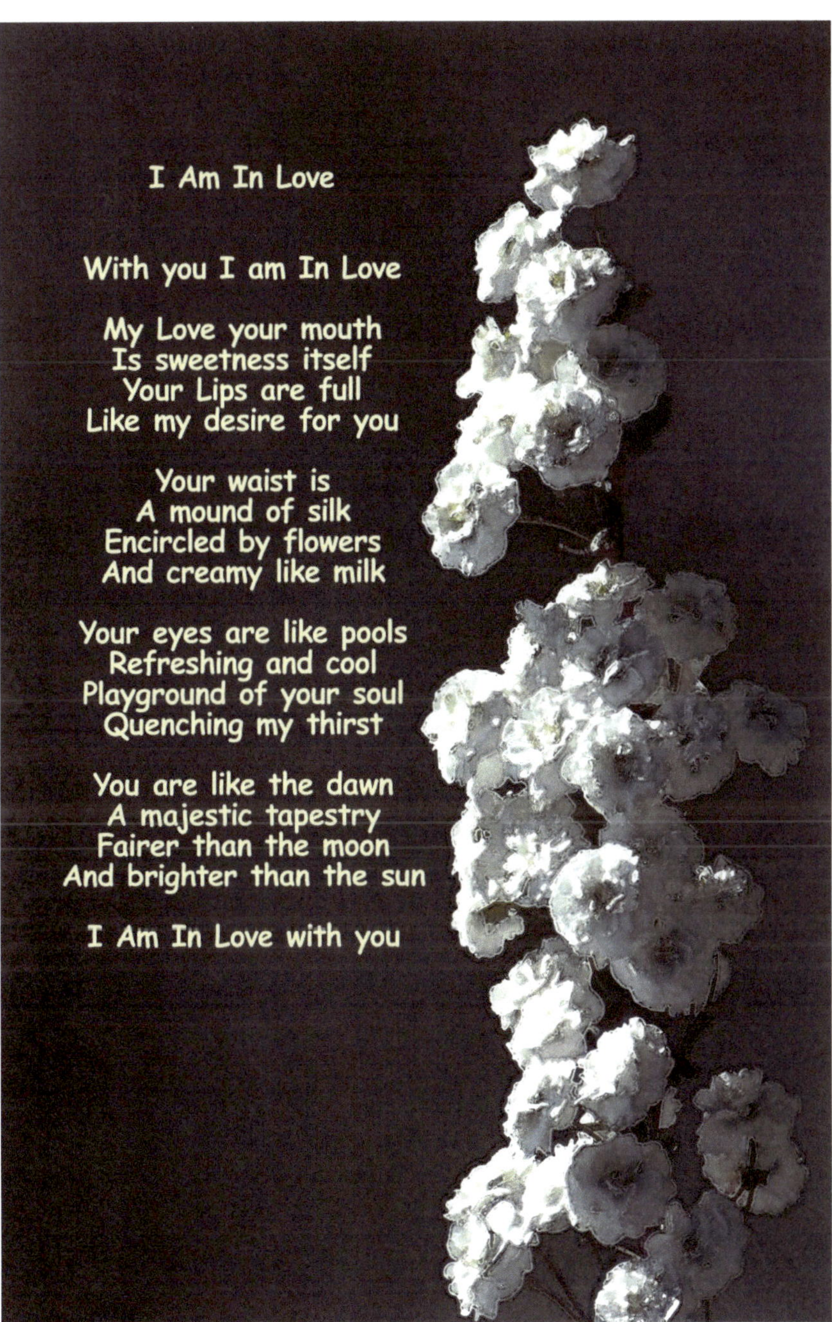
I Am In Love

With you I am In Love

My Love your mouth
Is sweetness itself
Your Lips are full
Like my desire for you

Your waist is
A mound of silk
Encircled by flowers
And creamy like milk

Your eyes are like pools
Refreshing and cool
Playground of your soul
Quenching my thirst

You are like the dawn
A majestic tapestry
Fairer than the moon
And brighter than the sun

I Am In Love with you

I Believe

I see your face My Love
Shining in the night time
You are far more beautiful
Than all the stars together

You smile in delight
Because shooting stars at night
Dance for you
You give each a twinkle

You point to the stars
But I can only see one
I see light in your eyes
To me you are the sun

Beautiful as they are
I believe
All the stars
Are your children

They Whisper to you in colors
Revealing themselves by name
Your Love gives them Life
And no two are the same

This is why you smile
Watching stars fly by
I see grace and beauty
Reflecting in your eye

Dr. Claus combines his love of poetry, photography, and nature to create art.

His published works include:

A Gift of Love
Parsifal
Love Poems 101
To Thee I Sing
Poems Of Love
The Promise
Daughter Of Kings
When You Breathe
My Love Whispers
The Poetess
Inhale Deeply
My Lover
Clair de Lune Serenade
My Gentle Butterfly
The Poetess (Aquarelle)
The Poetess (Luz Celestial)
The Promise (Aquarelle)
The Promise (Luz Celestial)
My Lover (Aquarelle)
To Thee I Sing (Aquarelle)
To Thee I Sing (Luz Celestial)
Inhale Deeply (Aquarelle)
Inhale Deeply (Luz Celestial)
The Keeper Of The Stones
My Love Whispers (Luz Celestial)
When You Breathe (Aquarelle)
Daughter Of Kings (Aquarelle)
Medley Mole Meets Buddy Rabbit
The Light Of The Trees El Corazon
Crumble Rumble Stumble Stew
Chuck Hug A Lunkle Ching Choo - Choo
A Hairy Scary Spider
The Day and Night before Christmas

www.ingramcontent.com/pod-product-compliance
Lightning Source LLC
LaVergne TN
LVHW052302100826
845147LV00001B/119

* 9 7 8 1 6 1 4 9 7 0 3 2 3 *